SUFI MEDITATION

Lights of Wisdom Series
No. 1

SUFI MEDITATION

LEX HIXON
NUR AL-JERRAHI

Pir Press • Westport, Connecticut

Pir Press
256 Post Road East
Westport, CT 06880

Published 1997
Printed in the United States of America

Library of Congress Catalog Card Number: 95-73253
ISSN 1091-1537
ISBN 1-879-70810-8

Maria Zerres created the cover design.

Calligraphy on back cover is the Çifte HÛ, a reflecting composition in jeli sulus script, drawn by Mohamed Zakariya.

SUFI MEDITATION

Members of the Noetic Science Association of New York City were studying meditation in various contexts and requested Sheikh Nur, the author and thinker Lex Hixon, to speak about what they called "Sufi meditation." On a weekday night, several of their members visited the beautiful third-floor music room of the Masjid al-Farah in southern Manhattan, where Sheikh Nur al-Jerrahi guided the Pir Nureddin al-Jerrahi dervish community for fifteen years. A spontaneous meeting of minds occurred, and this unusual discourse, taped on audio and later carefully edited and clarified by Sheikh Nur, was the result. Both dervishes and visitors were moved by the range, depth, and tenderness of these words as richly presenting Islamic Sufism and by the atmosphere of light that surrounded them on that special evening.

Sheikh Nur The preliminary for meditation is this: to establish a beautiful atmosphere. In Islam, there is no altar. We are the altar. There are no images of Divinity. We are the divine image. Human beings were created in the divine image. So now we are offering tea to this perfect image. We are seeing each other in a perfect light.

Visitor Noetic Sciences was founded by the astronaut Edgar Mitchell. On the way back from his trip into space, he had a realization that the universe is loving and intelligent and purposeful. His background gave him no preparation for this experience. Apparently, a number of the astronauts have had more or less similar experiences, but he decided to found an organization that would study the interface between science and spirituality. His background was scientific, and he wanted to see if there was some way that one could understand the connection between science and spirituality.

Sheikh Nur We will adopt that analogy. We are in an astronautical capsule right now. The universe is opening up above us, around us. All mystics of the great traditions have been astronauts into spiritual space and into physical space, because mystics walk through planetary experience, too, and perceive the Divine. They do not have to go to outer space or to inner space. They find sacred space everywhere. We are engaged in the countdown now. Instead of getting rocket engines prepared, we have to prepare the right kind of sweets, the right kind of tea, the right kind of fragrance, the right kind of friendship, the right kind of respect. All this is part of preparing for our lift-off.

I'm so glad to know the background of your Noetic Society. It's a large organization—tens of thousands of members, isn't it?

Visitor When I last heard, it was about forty thousand in various parts of the world.

Sheikh Nur That's quite a mystic order, forty thousand. Founded by a very modern person who had a profound spiritual experience. The founder of our order lived about three hundred years ago in Istanbul. He had extraordinary experiences, made possible by the spaceships that were available then.

Visitor Can you tell us about what happened to him?

Sheikh Nur Yes. He finished his extensive education in sacred law when he was about nineteen. He was already married. He had been appointed from Istanbul, which was the capital of the Ottoman Empire at that time, to go to Egypt and function as a Grand Mufti there, to give consultations on sacred law. The night before he was to leave, with everything packed and his passage on the ship secured, his uncle took him to a place like this, where you are tonight. The dervishes began chanting and whirling. Young Nureddin entered ecstasy. He took off his jacket and threw it in the center of the circle, which means he renounced his independent career and placed himself under the guidance of the sheikh. Everything was unpacked. His wife went to stay with her family, and he spent three years in intensive retreat.

When he was twenty-six, he had completed his total spiritual training, and his sheikh received the inspiration from Allah that Nureddin Jerrahi should start a new branch of the order. The young man, flanked by two supremely mature dervishes in their eighties, strolled a few miles from the tekke, the dervish lodge, into the center of Istanbul to found a new tekke. They had no money. They had nothing. The night before, the Sultan and also one vizier both had dreams that a young man flanked by two old sages would be coming into the city and would be founding a new mystic order, and that the state should open its coffers in order to give them funds. So the vizier went and easily found this configuration, one young man and two old men. They were just joyfully strolling. With the money that was provided they bought a beautiful old wooden house.

Sheikh Muzaffer Ashki, the nineteenth successor of Nureddin Jerrahi, arrived in New York in 1978. He similarly came with no particular money and no particular plan of how to establish a new tekke. He met the beautiful, radiant young couple who are sitting on either side of me right now. They are not as young as they were in 1978 but still as beautiful. They provided the means by which my Sheikh Muzaffer could establish the Jerrahi Order in New York City. That is the way it happens—spontaneously, by Divine Will.

This spontaneous unfolding is the secret, the art of meditation and of life. It is very personal. In the oral tradition of Islam, the Day of Judgment is described as the personal meeting of every soul with its Lord. It is not done with vast numbers of humanity stretching out beyond the horizons, and Divine Reality, as it were, sitting on a throne, judging. It is an individual, one-to-one, one-within-one experience.

Visitor Does it happen at a particular time?

Sheikh Nur It happens three times. The first time the Day of Judgment happens is every moment. The second time it happens is at one's physical death. The third time is at the culmination of history, when Being Itself will return into the glorious Source of Being. Those are three very real Days of Judgment.

I might add, a fourth time when it occurs is every Friday at the Friday prayers of Islam, which are called Juma, the gathering. That day, there is a reflection on earth of the cosmic Day of Judgment. A fifth time it happens is when the pilgrims on the pilgrimage to Mecca gather on the plain of Arafat. That is also a reflection in space and time of the cosmic Day of Judgment. The first three instances are metaphysical, and the other two are historical, earthly reflections.

The amazing thing about the Day of Judgment is that there is nothing but infinite Divine Mercy manifest on that day. There is no judgment as we understand it from any limited human standpoint. Allah says of Himself in the oral tradition, transmitted by His beloved Prophet Muhammad, upon him be peace, "My Mercy extends completely beyond My Justice." The Divine Quality of Justice is one of the facets of Supreme Reality, but the Divine Mercy extends infinitely beyond that. It is the essence of Supreme Reality. So the Day of Judgment is the day of infinite Mercy. In that Mercy, there can occur what we would consider chastening. There can be what we consider suffering, because people have to face themselves and be purified by the spiritual fire of Truth. Not physical fire. This Day of infinite Mercy is terrible in the sense that it can cause terror to the soul because it is such overwhelming mercy.

Dervish Farhad Fatima Sheikh Nur, do we meet the prophets on Judgment Day?

Sheikh Nur A beautiful question. On the Day of Judgment that happens at the time of physical death and on the Day of Judgment that happens at the End of Time, we do meet with all the prophets, upon them all be peace. All the saints and wise beings, both men and women who have been spiritual guides of humanity, also descend. The Cosmic Quran, which is to say the source of all the scriptures of the world, all the revealed principles, also descends. The earth of Judgment Day is a spiritual earth that can receive such manifestation, so intense that it would vaporize the physical earth. The bodies are spiritual bodies. All the human eyes that have ever gazed into creation, all the human nostrils that have ever taken grateful breaths of life-giving atmosphere on this planet—all these are resurrected, but in a spiritual sense, not in an ordinary, literal, physical sense. These are spiritual bodies, but they are very tangible.

This is not a subject I had thought of talking about tonight. It is just coming up spontaneously. In the Holy Quran, there is an interesting description of a particular soul who, when first awakening into the Resurrection, cries, "O Allah, please do not return me into my limited body." Our physical body, although it is an amazing body with tremendous spiritual reach, is limited. The soul is a limitless reality. This limitless reality cries, "Do not place me back inside limitation again." Allah replies in this Quranic passage, "Look at your body." The soul looks and sees that its body of resurrection is a body composed of light and love. In fact, it is a limitless body. Then the true mystery of the Resurrection begins to dawn on the soul, and the soul enters an ecstatic state of praise.

On the Day of Judgment that is appearing at every second we can also have this experience. We can experience our spiritual bodies. These spiritual bodies can appreciate fragrances and beautiful sights and tender touch. In Holy Quran, Allah says that the ones who pray sincerely and deeply will feel Divine Presence touching them through every pore of their skin—not just as a metaphysical presence, but as a direct touch.

Science fiction often depicts planet earth as some kind of prison planet. "If we were more evolved, we wouldn't be here." I have heard many New Age people say that. But that is not the Islamic view. This planet is at the very apex of spiritual possibility. The proof of this is that the beloved prophets have manifested here. The prophets are perfect, full human beings. Most prophets have rejoiced in marriage and in family, in food and drink. Most prophets have engaged in deep study and in sacred battle. The complete range of fruitful human experience and responsibility has been engaged in by these perfect human beings to show that there is nothing intrinsically limited here in our earthly life. We create limitations by our egocentric thinking, by our misapprehension. In the Day of Judgment that is happening at every moment, right here and now, we can know this limitless nature of our soul's experience. We can know the Resurrection.

This merciful Divine Judgment is happening right now within all of us. Look down at your body. It is composed of light. It is composed of love. It is not composed of what we theoretically and conventionally call matter. This experience is only for persons who can see metaphysically during earthly life. At the moment of our physical death, however, there is no avoiding this experience. Quran confirms this. We can avoid looking at our spiritual situation all our lives, but when the body is carried to the grave, then the soul has no recourse but to look at the situation fully. We do not have to wait for thousands or millions of years until the Day of Judgment at the End of Time. Definitely, at the moment of death, we will enter fully into that Day Without Evening.

I do not know what physical theory prevails right now, but according to some theories of the universe, there is an original expansion and then the universe contracts back into a single point. Metaphysically, this is the Quranic or the prophetic view. Creation is not just an endless dissipation into space. Creation has an actual rhythm to it. It reaches a certain point and then returns into its Source.

The Big Bang theory does not say anything about the Source. The Source is not something that can be investigated scientifically, so how can scientists talk about the Source? As human beings, however, we can and must talk about the Source. Creation returning into its Source is not a disappearing, a cancellation. It is the ultimate fulfillment of creation. So at that time, too, there will be a Day of Judgment—very grand, inconceivably magnificent.

The mystics are not confined by time, so they can experience that final return of Being into its Source here and now. They can experience their physical death before they die. Prophet Muhammad, may peace be upon him, often instructed his close companions, "Die before you die." This was originally a usage of the desert fathers of Christianity. The original form of the statement was, "Die before you die, and resurrect before the Resurrection." Can you imagine the ancient desert fathers saying that to each other? It is so beautiful. Instead of saying, "hello," one greets, "Die before you die," and the other responds, "Resurrect before the resurrection." Resurrect before the resurrection means that the mystic must experience within himself or herself that final Resurrection, even on the vast scale that it occurs at the end of history, including all living beings throughout space and time.

Now let's consider Sufi meditation, which is the subject requested by the Society of Noetic Sciences tonight. I have selected three passages from my book of meditations called *Heart of the Koran.* Everything in Sufism and Islam comes out of this root scripture, the Quran. You may have heard of Jelaluddin Rumi and other mystic Sufi poets. Their poetry is like a candle flame, and the Quran is like the sun. They would be the first ones to say this. The Holy Quran calls itself a hidden book. As the great Persian mystic Rumi wrote, "Quran is like a bride. She lifts her veil only for her husband." We are not like fundamentalists who claim,

"Everything is in the Torah, everything is in the Bible, everything is in the Quran." The fundamentalist position really is, "Everything is in this book, but you have to agree with me about what you find here." This is not the way to deal with holy scripture. Holy scripture is the most subtle of the subtle. Our Sheikh Muzaffer used to say that to study Quran is the highest mystical study. It should only be undertaken far into one's spiritual development, and it should be pursued under the guidance of one's sheikh, one's mystic guide. Quran study should never be undertaken merely from a scholarly standpoint, although scholarship about Quran, both in Islam and in the modern academic world, is very extensive and its findings are valid. But the mystical study of the Holy Quran should not be made through scholarship. It should be made through what we call unveiling. The meanings should be unveiled—exactly as Rumi suggests, like a bride unveiling herself to her husband.

I have selected three passages that I thought would shed light on what the Noetic Science Association calls Sufi meditation. I do not know what Sufi means or what meditation means, but I think that if we can find it anywhere, we can find it out from Quran.

Try to concentrate intensely as you listen. Although this is not the Arabic Quran, it is a mirror reflection of the Quran. This is not like reading from an earthly book. Experience these words as written on your hearts. As Saint Paul says about the Gentiles, they have the sacred law, the Torah, written on their hearts. The Holy Quran is found in the heart of humanity.

Sheikha Fariha reads:

Praise

> Whatever human beings say about reality, whatever advanced concepts they may hold, the Ultimate Source Who is now speaking will always be more exalted. All that is possible for any being is to praise Allah Most High, for none can describe Him. The very nature and function of Being Itself is to praise the Source and Goal of Being. The entire temporal universe, as well as the seven eternal realms and all the forms of consciousness they contain, are simply the living praise of the Ever-Present Source. To be is to praise Allah. Human beings fail to perceive this boundless praise arising spontaneously from all minds and hearts, or else they would understand instantly why such utter compassion and forgiveness flow to every being from the Source of Love.
>
> —meditation on *Holy Quran* 17: 43–44

Sheikh Nur Human conceptuality is an amazing gift. It allows us to discover various levels of reality. But it is extremely important for being truly human to know that our conceptuality has a limit. Whatever advanced concepts one may hold, "the Ultimate Source Who is now speaking will always be more exalted." The interesting point here is that the Source is speaking. The Source is affirming this limit to conceptuality. It is not human speculation. Here is the difference between philosophy and revelation. Each is fine in its own place, but revelation is obviously the crown. Our modern society is in danger of losing the whole overtone of revelation and staying with just philosophy and science.

"All that is possible for any being is to praise Allah Most High, for none can describe Him." The modern person may think, This is depressing. We want to describe God. We want to describe everything. All we can do is praise? That seems like a lower position. In this modern attitude our true priorities have been reversed. To praise is higher than to describe. It is a more exalted and magnificent experience. It is fuller, more satisfying, and more true. We should definitely describe what we can describe. We should not dogmatically claim that no one will ever be able to describe how the electrons circulate around the atom. Why not? Allow science to describe that through mathematics or through some other brilliant method of description. But we must always maintain our relationship with the Source, which is indescribable by its very nature, and we must praise that indescribability. If we fill our lives with description and have no praise, we will be anemic, personally and culturally, like having no iron in our diet.

The Quran takes us further into praise: "The very nature and function of Being Itself is to praise the Source and Goal of Being." I said earlier that creation is like an expansion and a contraction again to a point. The Source of Being is also the Goal of Being. The Source of Being is not something "way back there." The Source of Being is also the Ever-Present Goal of Being. Everything about Being is continuously returning into its Source. As it returns, it praises. In fact, its return itself is praise. This Quranic passage goes on to say, simply, "To be is to praise Allah." To be is to praise the indescribable Source of Being. So at this moment, just by being, we can consciously engage in universal praise. This is Sufi meditation. Just being! Our being itself is perfect praise. Of course, we are studying Quran together, so that study is also a form of praise.

All the hearts and all the minds in this room are now comprehending what I am saying. We are consciously participating in universal praise. Allah created the creation as a vehicle of praise, and we instinctively know this. "The entire temporal universe, as well as the seven eternal realms and all the forms of consciousness they contain, are simply the living praise of the Ever-Present Source. Human beings fail to perceive this boundless praise arising spontaneously from all minds and hearts." Praise is spontaneous. We cannot say to someone, "You are not praising enough." Praise is spontaneous and infinite. We cannot say, "Let's take a course on praising." It is spontaneous and unceasing, though of course we can attend a mystic order such as this one and learn to appreciate these spiritual facts. Praise is arising spontaneously from all minds and hearts in creation at this very moment. Teaching this, at this moment, I can feel my own awareness of universal praise expanding. The twenty million people around us right now in the New York City area are praising. Spontaneously. Whatever else they are doing. We do not have to take responsibility for whatever else they are doing; we can take responsibility only for what we are doing. But the fact is, they are all praising.

One can see how amazingly subtle this revealed book is. It has an almost playful way of turning back and expressing the same point from a different, surprising perspective. It says that if we truly perceived all this praise arising, we would not be surprised that infinite compassion and forgiveness are always flowing to every being from Allah, from the Source of Being. It is incorrect to think, "How kind Allah is! The universe and human beings are not praising Him, but He is still giving them sustenance and forgiveness." The universe is praising Him—completely and absolutely. Even the most negative persons, through their very being, are praising the Source of Being. Even though they may be extremely confused and walking in the wrong direction, there is always this core of praise—their very being itself. On the Day of Judgment, Allah will strip away all their negativity. It may be a painful experience, just as any bad habit, smoking, for instance, creates pain when it is first taken away.

Our next meditation on the Holy Quran will be more elaborate. There are many histories of prophets inside Quran. This passage is the enlightenment experience of the Prophet Abraham, upon him be peace. Those of you who are Jewish may know that a similar passage exists in Midrash, Jewish oral tradition.

Dervish Ahmed Munir reads:

The Enlightenment of the Prophet Abraham

The highest Truth, that the Ever-Present Source alone truly exists, was shown to the Prophet Abraham in this way. While he was immersed in solitary contemplation, within the vastness of the evening sky the first star suddenly appeared. To the pure vision of the Prophet, the star's light revealed the entire universe as the luminous manifestation of Allah's Majesty. While My intimate friend Abraham meditated on the bright mirror of My Creation, the evening star moved across the sky and disappeared behind the mountain. Perceiving this as clear teaching from the Source of Wisdom, he reflected: "Allah's Majesty cannot be loved as totally as one loves His Essence."

Then the full moon rose. Ascending further in contemplation, Abraham exclaimed: "Behold a mystic symbol for the transcendental beauty of Allah." But his meditation on Divine Beauty also came to an end as the moon disappeared behind the mountain. Recognizing once more a teaching from the Source of Wisdom, he prayed intensely: "Most precious Allah, please guide me beyond Your Majesty and beyond Your Beauty, or I will remain among those who do not awaken to the highest Truth."

Having supplicated the Supreme Source for guidance the whole night through, My intimate friend witnessed the magnificent desert sunrise. Perceiving the sun's vast radiance as a teaching from the Source of Wisdom, he declared: "Behold a mystic symbol for the Power of Allah." All day long he remained plunged in contemplation of Allah Most High as transcendent Power, but when the fiery sun finally set, his adoration of the Divine Attributes disappeared, and he awakened mystically into the Divine Essence alone.

—meditation on *Holy Quran* 6: 75–78

Sheikh Nur Abraham, upon him be peace, was undergoing an ascending series of spiritual experiences, sparked by the natural phenomena that surrounded him in his desert retreat. It is like the astronaut Mitchell. He was seeing the earth from the moon, a natural phenomenon, but it sparked something much more in him. It sparked the sense that the entire universe is loving and intelligent and purposeful. There is no way that just seeing a planet floating in space can create that experience. Mitchell saw the earth floating there as a Divine teaching. The noble Abraham did not have to fly to the moon to have this experience. He had it right on earth, as 124,000 prophets, upon them all be peace, and their families and followers have done throughout human history. It is we modern people who have become jaded with earthly experience. We have to go into outer space and look back to see earth as pure and sublime. Any particular way that Allah wants to show truth to us is good. One should not denigrate modern experience. But I want to emphasize that just seeing the physical phenomenon will not create the revelatory experience. We have to see the physical phenomenon as a radiant message or sign from the Source of Being. Then enlightenment explodes in our deepest awareness and we are taken to new levels of understanding.

The first level Abraham was taken to by Allah Most High was the contemplation of the evening star. This revealed to his purified vision that the entire universe is really the Divine Majesty. Maybe this is similar to the way astronaut Mitchell saw the whole universe as loving and purposeful. Gazing at this star opened the spirit of the Prophet so that he saw the entire universe as the perfect expression of Divine Majesty. He kept on contemplating the star and contemplating this transcendent fact. The star moved across the sky and disappeared behind the mountains. It took hours for this to happen, so the Prophet was in this state of Divine Majesty for hours. Probably Edgar Mitchell was in an exalted state of consciousness for hours as well, sitting in his capsule and looking out on earth. He saw that the universe was loving and purposeful—that is, the entire universe! He was not seeing that just this earth is loving and purposeful. His understanding extended far beyond to include the entire universe. This touches the edge of what the Prophet was experiencing.

When the star set behind the mountain, perceiving this as a clear teaching from the Source of Wisdom, Abraham reflected: "Allah's Majesty cannot be loved as totally as one loves His Essence." So the creation, as beautiful as it is, as purposeful as it is, cannot be loved as much as we love the Divine Essence, in other words, as we love the Source of Being out of which Being comes, out of which creation comes. Here is something that we modern people have not quite caught on to yet. We say, "I love the universe. It is purposeful. It is beautiful." But what we really love is the

Creator, the Source of the Universe. Through loving the universe, if our minds and hearts remain receptive, we can learn to love that Source. For the mystic, the universe becomes utterly transparent to its Source. The real object of our love is not the universe.

Abraham, however, was taking this much further. He was saying that one of the Divine Attributes, that of Majesty, cannot be loved as much as one loves the Divine Essence. It is hard for us to comprehend, but Abraham was actually going beyond the Divine Qualities, going beyond God as we can know Him, going beyond infinite Majesty. The Prophet was taken beyond.

Then the full moon rose. Abraham saw this also as a Divine Symbol, this time for the transcendental beauty of Allah. Beauty is more subtle than Majesty. Majesty involves all of this immense creation, but beauty can be found in a single flower, a single smile, or just the moonlight shining. Divine Beauty is much more delicate, much more elusive than Divine Majesty. The Prophet Abraham has now entered a much more subtle area of the Divine Attributes. Again, it is hard for you and me to understand these refinements, because what do we really know about the Divine Attributes? But this teaching is presented by the Holy Quran, so we have the responsibility to consider it deeply.

Lost for hours in the experience of Divine Beauty, Abraham suddenly saw the moon set behind a mountain. Recognizing this as a teaching from the Source of Wisdom, he prayed, "Most precious Allah, please guide me beyond Your Majesty and beyond Your Beauty, or I will remain among those who do not awaken to the highest Truth." We can now sense how spiritually radical a prophet is. If we ourselves had even a glimpse of Divine Majesty or Divine Beauty, we would be intoxicated for the rest of our lives. There would be no question of going beyond, of praying to Allah, "Take me beyond Your Divine Attributes." Abraham supplicated the Source of Guidance the whole night through. He did not think, "That was a wonderful experience. Now I'll take a few hours of sleep and wake for the dawn prayer." He went on supplicating, "Take me beyond! Take me beyond even Your Majesty, even Your Beauty!"

Finally, he perceived the intense radiance of the rising sun. He understood this as a symbol for Divine Power. He meditated the entire fourteen hours that the sun was in the sky. He did not contemplate the sun directly by staring at the physical manifestation. He meditated on Divine Power, which is totally inconceivable, by means of the sun regarded as a holy sign. We might say that Divine Majesty is somewhat conceivable and Divine Beauty somewhat comprehensible, but Divine Power points directly toward the inconceivable.

Then the sun set. This is when Abraham experienced enlightenment. He awakened into Divine Essence alone. It does not mean that moon, stars, and sun will never appear again or that the creation is somehow unreal. It does not mean that the mystic is ignoring Divine Majesty, Divine Beauty, and Divine Power. It means that the mystic has transcended both creation and Creator, plunging into the Source of these.

What happens when Abraham returns to his people? This is how it was revealed by Allah to the heart of His beloved Muhammad.

Dervish Ahmed Munir reads:

> After returning from the wilderness to his people, the Prophet Abraham proclaimed: "I have always been free from religious practices that exalt forces of nature. But now I have been brought face to face with the Essence of Allah, the Only Reality, Who alone radiates the broad expanse of earth and heaven. I have lost myself and found my Prophethood in the truth that Allah alone exists."
>
> The people disputed bitterly with their Prophet, threatening him with the wrath of the various etheric forces which they worshipped. Displaying the utter calm of illumination, Abraham replied: "Do you imagine that any threat or argument could turn me away from the Ultimate Source when I am experiencing direct guidance from the Source Itself? I fear no powers in the universe, for I have always turned toward the Source of

Power. Have you forgotten that the encompassing Awareness of Allah manifests and harmonizes the entire creation? How could I fear the hatred of any being when I am receiving constant inner assurance from the Source of Love? You are the ones who should be apprehensive, my people, having elevated your own limited concepts and experiences to the level of divinity. They can offer you no ultimate support or refuge. Consider carefully which of us is receiving true protection. Only those who turn solely toward the Source of Love and do not obscure their being by the slightest negation of Love are perfectly guided."

My beloved Muhammad, such was the illumined insight that the Source of Wisdom transmitted through the Prophet Abraham for the instruction of all humanity. The Ever-Present Source alone draws hearts and minds to higher and higher levels of vision and understanding. Allah Most High is encompassing Awareness and complete Wisdom.

—meditation on *Holy Quran* 6: 79–83

Sheikh Nur Enlightenment is simply to enter higher and higher levels of spiritual understanding. This is one of the passages in Quran that confirm the mystical path, the evolutionary way. Islam is a path, not just five pillars, not just the basic beliefs and practices. Even the noble Abraham was taken by Allah through different levels of spiritual experience.

The Prophet returned to the prophetic struggle, to warning and instructing his people. Prophecy is always rejected by people who are complacent, who wield power in society, who have some phobia about the sacred, or who are rigidly attached to some religious form, worshipping the way they saw their mother and father worshipping, refusing to develop, to transform. The prophetic consciousness always struggles with the people lovingly. The people seldom treat the prophet lovingly.

Enlightenment was transmitted by Allah to the Prophet Abraham for the instruction of all humanity. We are being instructed now by this revelation, fourteen centuries later, in New York City. We are being inspired by what was revealed to Abraham. More than that, we are being called to follow the ascending path of Abraham's own contemplation. This is Sufi meditation.

Visitor After meditating on the sun from sunrise to sunset, why was he enlightened?

Sheikh Nur He was enlightened not by meditating on the sun but by seeing the sun disappear, because he realized at that moment that no symbol, no image, not even any Divine Quality, can possibly be the reality that the Essence is, that the Source is. And he awakened as that Reality.

Visitor Was he finding the inner sun?

Sheikh Nur This was not just an external star Abraham meditated on. This was the inner star, the inner moon, the inner sun. Yet the Prophet discovered that there is a Reality beyond even the inner sun. This is the Source, the Essence, to which all creation is returning and which is the ultimate fulfillment of creation. Essence is not some blank, empty space. It is a supersaturated Reality, as Plotinus would say.

Are we not all profoundly honored to be with Abraham on his desert retreat, to go through the stages with him? You know how interesting it is to read retreat reports. Are we not astonished to be made intimate and contemporary with the noble Abraham's retreat experience? To be called to share it with him? Abraham is the father of Jews, Christians, and Muslims. There were no Jews, Christians, or Muslims in the time of Abraham. The spiritually awakened people were simply called hanifa, the upright ones, the true human beings. There was no organized religion. But I do not consider Judaism, Christianity, or Islam to be organized religions either. They are organic, organisms that spontaneously evolve. Some people try to organize or control what is spiritually spontaneous. These controllers appear in every generation and cause a certain amount of havoc, but they cannot destroy the organic power of revelation, because these organic revelations are Divine Creations, like sun, moon, and stars. Mao Tse-tung tried to control the life of the Chinese people, but could he proclaim that the sun will not rise and the moon will not shine? Similarly, in Russia, an oppressive regime tried to destroy religion, to destroy the viewpoint of revelation, to destroy the prophetic spirit. They were unable to do that. Even seventy years of revolution in Russia could not do that. Gorbachev himself was baptized. His grandmother secretly got him baptized when he was an infant. Nothing can destroy organic religion. Mao Tse-tung and oppressive, anti-religious Marxist regimes are actually a strange form of organized religion.

Visitor As Abraham meditated on the star and the moon and the sun, it filled his being with Presence, so when he had to go into the unknown, there was no fear. There is usually tremendous fear going to a place so completely unknown. Only when the whole being is full of knowing that Presence, can one go into the unknown.

Sheikh Nur A beautiful way of putting it. Now, as astronauts, we are ready for lift-off.

Sheikha Fariha reads:

Light

Calling Itself Allah, the Supreme Source is the One Light illuminating every heavenly and earthly realm. My beloved Muhammad, please transmit this profound meditation. The Light of Allah is the window that opens beyond all creation. On the sill of this shining window rests the precious lamp of the human soul, whose flame is pure and steady, protected by the transparent crystal of the heart that glistens delicately, like a star, with the soul's light. This lamp, ignited by Divine Love alone, burns aromatic oil from the Tree of Life, that transcendent Tree found nowhere on earth, neither in the East nor in the West. This fragrant oil of wisdom radiates illumination spontaneously, not needing to be touched by any earthly fire. Thus the light of the soul and the Source of Light behind it blend, merge, and reappear in the mystery of eternal companionship, as the Light of Allah within the Light of Allah.

Speaking thus to humanity through the most subtle figurative language, the Source of Wisdom guides to enlightenment whomever

It wills, for Allah is the One encompassing Awareness.

—meditation on *Holy Quran* 24: 35

Sheikh Nur Right here now, let's enter a meditation like the noble Abraham's meditation. We do not have to retire literally into the desert. We do not have to look literally to the evening star, because the crystal that surrounds the soul, the heart, glistens like a star.

The spiritual heart is the star we should contemplate, as Abraham did. With eyes open or eyes closed, whichever way we feel comfortable, let's consider this Quranic meditation on Light. Everyone who reads Quran is presented again and again with this very famous Sura of Light. We can be sure that Allah had us in mind—this particular room, these particular people—when this meditation was originally revealed, as well as all the others to whom this meditation will be presented until the end of cosmic experience, until the cessation of this planetary spaceship, until Allah brings physical creation to an end in some mysterious, unimaginable way.

We often think, We have no problem: we have another fifty million years of fuel in the sun. Quran never says that. Quran says that Allah can bring the universe to an end at any moment, perhaps during the night, when complacent persons are sound asleep. Being can be drawn back into the Source of Being at any moment. In our mystical order, we specialize in praying to Allah Most High to extend the universal earthly experience so that more and more souls will enjoy this precious spiritual experience of earthly embodiment—on habitable planets in all galaxies. This sacred earthly experience is really the highest spiritual evolutionary possibility. As I mentioned before, our earth is not a prison planet. It is not some unrefined netherworld. When we engage in Sufi meditation, we should never feel that we are low, or in a low place. Wherever we are is the most auspicious place. This mosque in New York City is just as good for Sufi meditation as the pristine desert where the noble Abraham made his retreat. This century is just as good as Abraham's century.

The Merciful, the Compassionate, the Beautiful, Allah: the Supreme Source calls Itself by these names and countless others. We do not feel that one Divine Name or another is required for Sufi meditation on the One Light. "Calling Itself Allah, the Supreme Source is the One Light illuminating every heavenly and earthly realm." It is not these electric lights that are illuminating this earthly realm right now, but the One Light. There is no distinction in Islam between the so-called material realm and the spiritual realm. That division is a peculiar modern concept, actually. We isolate matter, we define it as something mechanical, and then we insist that it is different from mind or spirit. "The One Light illuminating every heavenly and earthly realm." This One Light we are meditating on is right here now. Whether we close or open our eyes, it is here. "The Light of Allah is the window that opens beyond all creation." Finally, the noble Abraham's gaze went through that open window. At first he was seeing the arabesques, the shape of the window—reflections of Divine Majesty, Beauty, Power. This vast open window is the One Light. Do not imagine this light in some psychedelic sense. Please do not engage in some fantasy that maybe the radiance in this room will start growing brighter and brighter. That is not what is meant by the One Light, the window that opens beyond all creation.

"On the sill of this shining window rests the precious lamp of the human soul." We are right now at rest on the sill of that window. It is not someplace far away. We should not think, Maybe we will get there someday. Our soul is an oil lamp "whose flame is pure and steady," resting on the sill of that magnificent window right now. Our minds may not be entirely pure and entirely steady, but put that aside. We are experiencing the soul now, not the mind. The soul's flame is pure and steady right now and eternally. It does not need any meditative technique. We do not need to steady the soul by breathing slowly or sitting up straight. We cannot do anything for the soul. We do not need to do anything for the soul. The soul's light is pure and steady. We should at least know that, and perhaps we will experience it directly. Why not? It is our own true light. Why shouldn't we be able to experience it?

This flame is "protected by the transparent crystal of the heart that glistens delicately, like a star, with the soul's light." Go initially in the direction of the physical heart. Jewish and Islamic mystics and also Christian desert fathers and mothers used to meditate, not like yogis with head straight up, but with head slightly bent, inclining down toward the left-hand side of the chest, gazing in the direction of the physical heart. That is only the direction. Obviously we are meditating not on a certain physical organ that is pumping and giving life but on a spiritual organ that is pulsing with light and giving spiritual life. We are meditating on the spiritual heart. If you feel it might help, incline your head downward to the left in the direction of the physical heart, close your eyes, and see the star. At first you will see a vast black space, and then maybe you will see a star like the evening star that the noble Abraham saw. That star is the spiritual heart, which is really like a transparent crystal surrounding the steady flame of the soul. The crystal is glistening, as stars do. It is very dynamic. The soul's light is a steady flame, but extremely subtle and difficult to find. The heart's light is a glistening. It is easy to find. We can pick it out in the vast sky of awareness. See that star, and then go through that star. After all, the star is just a crystal surrounding the soul's light. Go through that star as Abraham went through star, moon, and sun, and enter the steady, pure flame of the soul. The essential flame.

"This lamp, ignited by Divine Love alone." This lamp has been lighted, according to Islam, since before there was any universe in the first place. In Islam, souls are eternal in both directions. This lamp of the human soul was ignited before there were even angels, before there was even a Divine Throne. In preeternity, as Islam puts it, this lamp was ignited. But what was it ignited by? There was nothing to ignite it but Divine Love. "This lamp, ignited by Divine Love alone, burns aromatic oil from the Tree of Life." This is why we put a little fragrant oil on your hands earlier this evening. There is an aromatic dimension to Sufi meditation. The soul's light has a perfume. Experience that also.

"Aromatic oil from the Tree of Life, that transcendent Tree found nowhere on earth, neither in the East nor in the West." Let's not run to the East to study religion. Let's not run to the West to study science or religion. Let's not run any place in the world to study. This Tree of Life, which provides oil for the soul's lamp, is not found in the East or the West. This fragrant oil is not some material oil, not some cultural form. It is wisdom. "This fragrant oil of wisdom radiates illumination spontaneously, not needing to be touched by any earthly fire."

At this point, I think everyone has the meditation clearly in mind and heart. Please do not feel that you have to visualize all this, as if it were a videotape. Just understand what is going on. This is a meditation of truly understanding the human being. This Quranic passage is describing every human being. It is not a meditation only for an elite group. In every single human being on the planet, this meditation is actually going on, no matter how veiled these persons might be, how unhappy or confused they might feel. Sometimes each of us feels unhappy or confused, and we forget this spiritual fact, this One Light, which is our real nature. We do not need to begin Sufi meditation. It is always going on.

Next comes the meditation proper. What has come before is the setting for the diamond. "Thus the light of the soul and the Source of Light behind it blend." Our souls are not confined to a place, even an exalted place on the sill of this radiant window that opens beyond all creation. Our soul's light can actually blend with the Source of Light. Now feel that blending. "The light of the soul and the Source of Light behind it blend and merge." Merging is one step further than blending. To merge means to experience identity with that Ultimate Source. Then the most wonderful thing: to reappear. "The light of the soul and the Source of Light behind it blend, merge, and reappear in the mystery of eternal companionship." This is not some nirvana situation, where you blend, merge, and that's it. The ultimate evolution is that we reappear and manifest the mystery of eternal companionship—the companionship between soul and Lord, eternal bride and eternal bridegroom, lover and beloved in Sufi imagery. "Blend, merge, and reappear in the mystery of eternal companionship, as the Light of Allah within the Light of Allah." Our soul's light is no longer seen as some separate reality. It is the Divine Light. We are the play of the Divine Light within the Divine Light. It remains very important in Islamic mysticism that the uniqueness of the soul's light is never swallowed up in infinite Light. Our unique light plays eternally in the play of Divine Companionship. This is not a mysticism of total reabsorption, like the raindrop reabsorbed into the ocean. Such is not Islamic mystical teaching. Sufi meditation is much more exalted than total absorption.

"Speaking thus to humanity through the most subtle figurative language." This sole scripture of Islam, this Holy Quran, is fourteen centuries old. These words were received through inspiration by an Arabian man who was brilliant but not literate in the sense of extensive reading and writing. There were no universities in Arabia at that time. Yet this certainly is the most subtle, figurative language. I have never encountered any teaching more subtle than this. I am not saying that this scripture is the only one or the best one. I am just saying that we have to recognize its subtlety. We have to stand in awe of this Quranic meditation. No sacred tradition gets any subtler than this. "Speaking thus to humanity." This wonderful

Divine Speaking is for us, here and now. "Speaking thus to humanity through the most subtle figurative language, the Source of Wisdom guides to enlightenment whomever It wills, for Allah is the One encompassing Awareness."

We might be tempted to say, "Let's sit quietly for twenty minutes and meditate on this," but I do not think that would be real Sufi meditation. Why? Because that would imply we can get close to our soul's light while we are quiet for twenty minutes or one hour and the rest of the time we are far from it or barely conscious of it. Most people think, We are handling practical affairs and really don't have time for meditation. The Sufis do not accept that. This awareness of the One Light, this "One encompassing Awareness," can be perpetual in one's life, even in conjunction with all the sorrows and efforts we go through. That is why I will not say, Sit for twenty minutes and meditate. That would subtly enforce a sense of separation between meditation and living itself.

Of course, it will be helpful sometimes to make a retreat or to recall this meditation when one is in solitude. After all, if the Prophet Abraham went into retreat, it is good for us, too. But we need not do that now.

I think all of us, including myself, have never understood this spiritual situation so clearly. I am not giving a lecture. I am not an old college professor whose lecture notes are yellow with age. This is not an address that I have given for the last twenty years to the freshman class. I have never presented Sufi meditation this way before. It has never been so clear to me. This is because of the goodness and the intensity of the people who are here. It is you that brought it through.

Let's not make a distinction between outside and inside. Let's not say that we have to "go inside." We don't, because two of the principle ninety-nine Divine Names are the Outer and the Inner. Divine Reality is everywhere we look. Close your eyes or open your eyes—it doesn't make any essential difference. It may make a difference to some people, but only as a question of temperament.

Dervish Medina You were saying that the light of the soul and the Light of Essence merge and then reemerge. In the state of eternity, is there still companionship?

Sheikh Nur Yes. Reality is a play of companionship. Medina is really asking about the essence of Sufism here: this eternal companionship, this Divine Play. Strange and wonderful things can happen in this play. For example, our Sheikh used to say that the greatest lovers of Allah, ones who are most intimate with Divine Reality, who have been consciously established in this eternal companionship, refuse to enter Paradise until all other beings enter Paradise. They bring pressure on God. They do amazing things. We sing in one of our mystic hymns: "The holy friends are past description, their ways are manifold."

Part of the play is that every soul is unique. There is nothing mechanical or repetitive about the infinite Divine Creativity. Each of Allah's creations is unique. Each moment of creation is unique. Imagine the play that is going on between countless souls and their Lord, all of them unique, none of them separate.

Our Sheikh used to say that a single tear from a saint of love can put out the fires of hell. Not that Allah is interested in perpetuating hellfire, but there is no way He can permit the fires of hell to burn, because His playful companions are continuously weeping out of love and putting out the fires of negativity as they spring forth again and again.

I refer to this as the mystery of eternal companionship. It really is a mystery. You will find this mystery in the lives of saints and sages from all sacred traditions—this unique play, this unique interaction, which is not described in any textbook on religion and which is never happening the way it is "supposed to happen." In Russian Orthodox Christianity, there are fools for Christ, special beings who appear to be mad on the surface but who are engaged in an inner play with the Divine. Their madness is just a cloak or veil for great inner sanctity. We do not have to be saints or mystics. We can be just the ordinary people we are, yet our lives are secretly engaged in this Divine Play.

Sometimes the play resembles hide and seek. Allah is successfully hiding from many modern people. But that is also part of the play. If Allah wanted to reveal Himself and make modern humanity suddenly devout, it is perfectly possible for Him. But He wills to play hide and seek. It is the lover's play with the beloved. Allah is love itself. Who could be a more subtle lover than love itself? A prominent Quranic name for Divine Reality is the All Subtle, in Arabic, Latif. What could be more exalted than to play with a Reality that is infinitely subtle?

Some people imagine that eternity might be boring. They say, "I can deal with time, because things change." We imagine eternity in various childish ways, like staring endlessly at the Divine Throne. We should not rely on our imagination but seek guidance from revelation. Because of this play of eternal companionship, eternity is dynamic. Paradise is described by the Holy Quran—these are symbolic descriptions, yet they are spiritually valid—not as sitting around and gazing at the Divine Throne, or at God, in rapt beatific trance. Paradise is a huge fiesta, a banquet where lovers are facing each other, sitting at long banquet tables filled with the food and drink of wisdom and love. Quran reveals that the souls in Paradise are answering each other's most burning questions with the Divine Wisdom Itself. The Divine Playmate is manifesting right through each soul in Paradise. There, our play with the Divine becomes our play with other souls. Anything that can be experienced in Paradise can also be experienced here on earth, which is simply the reflection of Paradise in the mirror of the heart—clear or distorted, depending upon our purity of heart. Our love-play with another human being on earth can become love-play with the Divine.

Dervish Medina What about the Abode of Essence?

Sheikh Nur This is very important. We have a teaching that one goes beyond Paradise. Just like the noble Abraham, we go beyond the realm of Divine Names, which is Paradise, this realm of Magnificence, Beauty, Power, Subtlety. Abraham begged Allah to take him beyond all that. This journey into Essence does not cancel out Paradise, however. That is a false idea we have to be careful about. Some people take our Sufi essence-teaching that way and conclude that Paradise is just a dream, that we are going to transcend those banquet tables, those ecstatic conversations, those whirling circles of souls that are Paradise. "That's a lower understanding," such persons say. "We're going to the Abode of Essence." Such is not our way. One goes beyond Paradise only to come forth again as Paradise. One becomes Paradise. One is no longer simply in Paradise. One is Paradise. We sing of Fatima, the daughter of Muhammad the Messenger, upon him be peace, as "the living essence of Paradise." One becomes this essence. As we read in the Quranic meditation, one merges in order to reemerge as the Light of Allah within the Light of Allah. Unless we merge our personality structures, and even our very sense of individuality, in the Essence, then we cannot come forth as the Divine playing within the Divine. We cannot really become master players. The mystic merging is necessary, but it is the penultimate step. The ultimate step is to manifest again as the realm of multiplicity, whether it be heavenly or earthly. One is then shining forth as that creative play of the Divine Names, the rays of Divine Light.

This teaching is not new. One of the great archbishops of Constantinople, Saint John Chrysostom, lived around the fourth century of the Christian Era, before the Prophet Muhammad, upon him be peace, manifested on the earth, before there was a single Muslim Sufi on earth. Someone asked the holy bishop, "Is your soul going to Paradise when you die?" He replied, "I am not interested in going to Paradise, for I have become Paradise." Clear realization. Clear Sufism before the word *sufism* existed. This is the mystery. As we sometimes say in our prayers, "May the veils of soul and Lord melt away in supreme identity." Then soul and Lord reemerge as total, indivisible Divine Manifestation.

We are partially veiled by our sense of separation from the Divine. When we begin to blend, that is the spiritual path. We are actually in the blender right now, or we would not be speaking together like this.

Eventually, when we merge, then all veils dissolve and we come forth as unveiled essential creation. At that point, creation has simply ceased to be a veil. Even the mysterious companionship of soul and Lord is no longer a veil over the Garden of Essence. It is all essence. It is all essential.

Dervish Medina So it is all eternal life.

Sheikh Nur Yes, eternal life. The beloved Jesus, upon him be peace, once said, "Whoever accepts me"—in other words, whoever accepts my blending, my merging, my reemerging—"has already passed from death to life." The spiritual lovers of Jesus are already in eternal life. All the sacred traditions present this possibility. That is what constitutes a religious tradition—precisely this possibility. Sufis don't have a corner on the market. This is what not only religion but life itself is all about. Of course, the spiritual facts are expressed in such different ways that sometimes we wonder, Is this religion the same as ours or not? Allah's infinite Creativity is so creative! Sometimes we can barely recognize the Divine Play, unless we become essential ourselves. If we become essential, we recognize the Divine Play everywhere.

We used to take our Sheikh Muzaffer to the Tavern on the Green in Central Park on pleasant afternoons. We would sit at the outside tables, drink tea, and eat chocolate cake. Some people would be walking through the park with big boom boxes. We'd think, "They're ruining this beautiful scene. We have our grand sheikh here, we're in Paradise, and these people are coming in and blasting Paradise." We would look over at Muzaffer Efendi and he would be chanting to the rap music, "Hayy, Hayy, Hayy . . . ," Arabic for the Ever-Living One, his body moving gracefully as in a Sufi dhikr, or circle of Divine Remembrance. He was existing in an unveiled creation. We still have veils over us. We sing in one of our mystic hymns: "Nothing exists that veils the face of Truth. This is the teaching of every mystic guide." In the Middle East, in the Far East, among the Native Americans, wherever there are mystic guides, this is what they are ultimately teaching. We are already eternal life. There is no actual veil. The veils are something that we generate. Allah does not generate them. Reality does not generate veils, but we misperceive, and our very misperception becomes a veil.

However, it would be a further misperception of our misperception to think of it as some sort of substantial veil, as if we have to pull something away to see the face of Truth. Let's not add misperception to misperception. Let's say, "Okay, we've misperceived Reality right now. We don't think that we are looking directly at God, but we really are." We do misperceive Divine Reality as some form of limited world and limited self, but let's not also misperceive our misperception by insisting that there is a thick veil here and that we have to get through it somehow, as if it were a dense miasma. The true teaching of Sufism and Vedanta is that there is no substantial maya. Maya, Sanskrit for dualistic illusion, is a misperception, a misreading of experience. It is not a big fog covering Reality. There is no maya. All this is God. All this is Reality.

Dervish Rabia Rachel Wadud What is the difference between the person who has become essential and one who has not?

Sheikh Nur There is no difference. There is only essentiality. The Zen masters say, "I am exactly like any ordinary human being." They mean it. It is not false humility. They see every actual human being as an enlightened Buddha, which they are.

Because the Noetic Sciences people are here tonight, I am mentioning imagery from other sacred traditions. Usually, I don't do that. Let's stay with the Quranic references, which are complete in themselves.

Visitor When did Muhammad live? Did Muhammad and Abraham live at the same time?

Sheikh Nur Abraham lived maybe two thousand years before Jesus. Muhammad, upon him be peace, lived around the year 600 of the Common Era. But Abraham and Muhammad were twin brothers. Both believed in one universal religion rather than in separate religions.

We adore Muhammad, upon him be peace, because he received the Holy Quran and is still helping us spiritually. He thought that sincere Jews and Christians would join with him. He did not think he was starting another religion. He thought it was very peculiar to separate different religions coming from the same root of Abraham. There are many people today who belong consciously to the universal religion of Abraham. They cannot see any essential distinction between Christianity, Judaism, Islam, and other noble traditions. The Prophet Muhammad was like Abraham—just an upright person who did not think that he was founding a separate religion but was, by Allah's decree, simply pointing out the one universal religion, as all the Messengers have done. Allah reveals in the Quran, "I have sent a messenger to every nation in history, bearing the same essential message." There is no invisible border at the Mediterranean and on the far side of Syria beyond which no prophet has ever appeared. Every spiritual nation in history has received at least one prophet. Universal religion is that seamless prophetic vision of human history as already fully immersed in Divine Reality, however it may be expressed by different cultures.

I think such understanding would appeal to a modern individual. Perhaps the teaching of Prophet Muhammad may be especially relevant for a planetary civilization. He was a planetary person living before there was any genuine planetary civilization.

Muhammad and Abraham were both convinced by God that there is only one religion. At a certain point in the Islamic daily prayers, we ask Divine Peace to descend upon Abraham and Muhammad. We single out these two Messengers in particular. You had an intuitive sense about that. They did not have historical contact, but they do have important inner contact.

Visitor When our soul leaves our body and we are in the gardens of Paradise, is there a community where we help one another again, or is it exclusively an experience with Allah?

Sheikh Nur Certainly souls commune with one another in Paradise. They answer each other's burning questions. Paradise is a communal experience. The picture of Paradise revealed by Quran is not individual yogis sitting in trance and communing only with Allah. The souls are seated together at spiritual banquets and drink together from spiritual springs. There is deep mutuality in Paradise consciousness. There is eternal companionship. Since there is no physical time in Paradise, there is no morning prayer or evening prayer. There is no sun in Paradise. Everything is radiating its own mystic light. But even without a temporal form of prayer, there is communion. There are dervish dhikr circles in Paradise. The circles of Divine Remembrance in Paradise are amazing. The inner circle is composed of the 124,000 prophets, with the

Prophet Muhammad, upon him be peace, taking the role of the sheikh. That is just the inner circle. Around it circle all the mystic saints, and around them, all the other lovers, and around them anyone who loved any of these human beings.

I was studying the Prophet's oral tradition today. He reported something wonderful directly from Allah Most High. Allah has angels that go looking for gatherings just like this one we are experiencing right now, circles of Divine Remembrance—speaking about Divine Reality, invoking Divine Reality, contemplating Divine Reality, expressing Divine Reality. When an angel finds a place like this, he calls to the other angels, "Come to witness!" The angels come and surround this earthly circle of lovers, and their angelic wings extend into the heavenly realms. Allah now tells the angels, "You are My witnesses. I forgive and absolve everyone in this circle because of their intensity, because of their love." One of the angels objects, "But Allah . . ."

Angels can speak only from their angelic intelligence, which is limited. Human beings are much more exalted than angels. This is the teaching of both the Eastern Orthodox Church and Islam. Our task is not to become like angels. Our exalted spiritual task is to become true human beings, who have a higher station than angelic beings. Human beings are intimate in the Divine Play. Angels do not play with Allah. Angels are very serious. They do not taste the ecstatic union with Essence. They whirl around the throne and bring messages to the planetary plane. They are obedient and loving, but they do not have our potential spiritual subtlety. They cannot have the experience of merging with Reality and reemerging as eternal Divine Companions, as Light within Light. They are creations. The human soul, in an essential sense, is not a creation.

So the angel objects, from his limited angelic intelligence, "But Allah, there is a person in this circle who is not really part of these people. He came for a different purpose, with some other agenda." Allah replies, "Everyone in this circle is part of the circle." That covers us. We may think, I came here for another reason. Perhaps all of us do not feel that our motivation in coming here tonight was pure love or pure longing for truth. Maybe our mind was wandering. Maybe we do not think we are really part of all this. But Allah sees us as part of the circle. The people of remembrance, the Sufis who make these circles of Divine Remembrance, gather all their friends and loved ones, not only physically but spiritually. For instance, right here and now, all our parents are with us, whether they are still on earth or their souls have passed to the next world. Why? Because our parents are spiritually inseparable from us. They are always with us. Since we are thinking of them, consciously or unconsciously, they are here. Our friends, everyone our hearts are joined with, are together with us in this circle tonight.

If you look in this room at this circle, it appears rather small, but if you add all family, all loved ones, and all people whose hearts are genuinely connected with everyone in this room, we would have more than a stadium full of people. This is what the sacred circle is. Allah says, "I forgive everyone in this circle for their intensity and their love." You Noetic Sciences people do not have to come back here. The blessing is not incremental. One does not have to attend every week in order to be forgiven and transformed.

Sheikha Fariha Each one will find happiness?

Sheikh Nur Not a single person in this room will fail to achieve complete fulfillment. It's not that some are along for the ride and will receive only a partial blessing. No. Everyone here will achieve complete fulfillment. All of humanity is circling around the Messengers. We are all part of the circle of Abraham, the circle of Moses, the circle of Jesus, the circle of Buddha, the circle of Krishna. This has already been accomplished by Allah. This is Allah's infinite Mercy. No amount of human stubbornness and stupidity can impede infinite Mercy.

Dervish Farhad Fatima When souls meet and talk to each other and commune with each other, is there gender?

Sheikh Nur Physical gender is like the star and moon Abraham saw. The star indicated magnificence, and the moon indicated beauty. So let's say that masculine physical gender might indicate certain divine qualities and feminine physical gender might indicate certain other divine qualities, or different configurations of the same qualities. Everything in the so-called physical universe is a living symbol, a teaching about what is beyond. In this biological existence, our gender is a teaching and a symbol of something beyond. There is also gender in Paradise. Of course, it is not biological gender. It is a spiritual quality that remains without any biological implications but with implications for ecstatic love and union and the special relationship between souls. It is hard to imagine Paradise. Since all the souls there are facets of one infinite diamond of Awareness, we might say that all souls in Paradise are married to each other, and they experience the delight of union that in earthly life husband and wife experience together. Quran says that the delight experienced by lovers on earth is a mirror reflection of the delight experienced in Paradise. Any genuine Tantric practitioner will tell you that. Gender and sexuality are symbols for much greater levels of experience. There are husbands and wives in Paradise, but it is not an exclusive relationship, as it is on earth, and it is certainly not a biological relationship, yet it manifests much more intense delight than its earthly counterpart.

Basically, everything that is of value on earth—every structure of value—is recreated or re-manifested in its essentiality in the realm of Paradise. If when you were twelve years old you happened to be walking in the woods one winter and saw a rabbit crossing a fresh field of snow and it looked pure and pristine and free and you remember that and cherish that, it will be in Paradise. This does not mean there will be snow in Paradise or a rabbit. The essential reality of that experience will be in Paradise. Allah willing, every human being that you have known intimately and loved will be in Paradise in an essentialized, purified way.

Paradise is not just a little garden somewhere. It is not a story to tell children. It is a vast expanse of all the moments, structures, and beings of value that have ever manifested in time anywhere in the universe. That is really what Paradise is. The Prophet, upon him be peace, reported that the Archangel Gabriel once flew upon his wings of unobstructed intuition—these are not physical wings—the Archangel once flew in every direction to find the border of Paradise and could not find it. That is how big it is. The Prophet walked over the far boundary of Paradise and stepped into the Garden of Essence. This is what all of us must do. This is why human beings are higher than angels and archangels. Angels cannot even find the border of Paradise, whereas we human beings have to go to that border and cross it.

Archangel Gabriel was with the Prophet, upon him be peace, at that ultimate moment of crossing during his mystic night journey, his miraj, because the Archangel was always with the Prophet. They were inseparable companions, beloved companions. Miraculously and suddenly, by Allah's Permission and Mercy, the Prophet reached the edge of Paradise, which the Archangel could never find on his own. Then the Archangel addressed the Prophet: "I cannot cross that boundary, because I am part of creation. That is beyond creation. Paradise is still part of creation. I cannot go across that boundary. I would be incinerated. I do not have the Divine Permission. I am a creation, but you, O Muhammad, are the very embodiment of the Divine Essence." All human beings are the Divine Essence breathed by Allah into the most beautiful form. Muhammad, upon him be peace, never suggested that he was structurally different from any human being. The Archangel proclaimed, "You are the embodiment of the Divine Essence. That is your homeland over there. Go!" The Prophet did not remain in the Garden of Essence, however. He went and he came back again as Mercy to the Worlds. That is the whole point of Islamic mysticism or Sufi meditation. One does not remain in the Garden of Essence. One merges and then reemerges as the Divine Energies, or Attributes, in the beautiful play of eternal companionship.

Visitor Are Paradise and the Garden of Essence separate?

Sheikh Nur Yes. Two different planes of reality, let's say.

Visitor Is Paradise unlimited?

Sheikh Nur Paradise is unlimited from the perspective of the Archangel. Gabriel cannot find the limit of it. But it is limited, because there is an end to it, because it is a creation. Allah created it. Creation is not infinite. Only the Source of Creation is infinite, although creation mysteriously mirrors the infinity of its Source.

Visitor So creation is a certain limited area. Can you bound it? Can you measure it?

Sheikh Nur Well, if Archangel Gabriel could not find its limit, we might have trouble doing so. Certainly, the scientists will not be able to bound or measure creation with their empirical tools or their mathematics. But the point is that the Prophet, by Allah's permission, could do it. He was representing all human beings. Our calling is not just to Paradise. This is a misunderstanding. "All I want is Paradise. Get me out of this world." This is not the Sufi attitude. Paradise is a stepping stone to the Garden of Essence, which is our true home, but we immediately come forth again from that state of merging and are manifest subtly throughout all planes of being in companionship with all beings and the radiant Source of Being.

Visitor When you die, you go to Paradise?

Sheikh Nur Unfortunately, when persons die they can go to some illusory places that they have dreamed up themselves through their own discord and negativity—bizarre, terrible, deceptive places. The Quran calls this the experience of hellfire.

Dervish Medina After the merging into Essence, there is the reemerging into the state of Paradise. Paradise is created. How can the soul, which has merged with Essence, reenter creation?

Sheikh Nur The soul becomes Paradise. It is not really reentry. When the soul merges, there is no more soul and Lord. There is only Supreme Reality. Supreme Reality is manifesting right now as the earth-plane and as the Paradise-plane. Supreme Reality is not "entering" creation. There is only Supreme Reality.

Dervish Medina But you said before that the light of the soul and the Light of the Essence still coexist at that point.

Sheikh Nur Yes, but this coexistence is a play that the Divine alone is performing. The Divine is transparently playing as soul and Lord. We now no longer imagine that we are separate souls engaging in this play of coexistence. There is a subtle difference here from souls on the spiritual path who are seeking their Lord or even meeting their Lord. This nondualistic coexistence is our deeply sought Sufi meditation.

This dervish meeting hall is a laboratory. We are much more advanced here in our considerations than the most advanced atomic physicists or the most advanced mathematicians. We are discussing here dimensions that are way beyond the ken of their disciplines. They are wonderful people and are doing good work, but we have to be honest about this difference in level. We are presenting here a level that only the most exalted revelation touches. We are not patting ourselves on the back and saying, "Aren't we great." We are simply saying, "Isn't it wonderful that normal human beings like us can sit together and talk about this!" We cannot really talk about the depth of modern physics unless we spend ten years studying advanced mathematics. But any human being, through scriptural guidance, can comprehend the deep nature of Creation, Paradise, and Essence, which is infinitely more advanced than the study of physics or mathematics.

Our meeting tonight is like being companions in the circle around the Prophet Muhammad, upon him be peace. This is just the kind of spiritual discussion they held together in the ancient desert of Arabia. This process of deep questioning is exactly what the Hadith, the oral tradition of Islam, came out of. Our discussion is not one bit less profound, because we are basing it on Quran and Hadith. This moment is revelatory. We do not usually speak of our evenings here this way, because we do not think about it, we just do it. But since the Noetic Science Association is visiting, we looked at it for a second from your eyes. Tonight is not an introduction to Sufism; it simply is Sufism. This is why we decided to meet here. This is why I did not come to your place. I thought, "Why not bring them to the mosque? Bring them to the laboratory and show them the way we work." Now you see what we are investigating. Now you feel it for yourselves. This is total Sufism.

Visitor It has been a wonderful experience.

Sheikh Nur For us, too. You bring something special. All of you. You bring a presence and a vibration of something very pure. Our Sheikh Muzaffer Ashki, who passed away from the surface world in 1985, would be overjoyed to meet with you and talk with you because he was interested in introducing Islamic Sufism on a universal plane, not in a ghetto situation with Muslims here, Christians over there, Jews over there, and atheists over there. He wanted to introduce Islamic Sufism in a way that would be accessible to everyone who had the heart, not as a segregated religion. He would be very happy to meet all of you. Through me, he is meeting you tonight and you are meeting him.

Masjid al-Farah
October 10, 1994

The Islamic writings of Nur al-Jerrahi (Lex Hixon)—Heart of the Koran *(Quest Books, 1988) and* Atom from the Sun of Knowledge *(Pir Press, 1993)—as well as the writings of his Sheikh, Muzaffer al-Jerrahi, are available from Sufi Books, 227 West Broadway, New York, NY 10013, phone (212) 334–5212, fax (212) 334–5214.*